D0996839

msc

PROPAGANDA

STEWART ROSS

Wayland

PROPAGANDA

Titles in this series

Propaganda
The Women's War
Victims of War
World Leaders

Cover illustration: German propaganda aimed at inspiring young people to support Hitler.

First published in 1993 by
Wayland (Publishers) Limited
61 Western Road, Hove
East Sussex BN3 1JD, England

Series editor: Paul Mason
Designers: Malcolm Walker/John Yates

British Library Cataloguing in Publication Data
    Ross, Stewart
    Propaganda. – (Era of the Second World War)
    I. Title II. Series
    940.54

ISBN 0-7502-0777-9

Typeset in the UK by Dorchester Typesetting Group
Printed and bound in Italy by Rotolito Lombarda S.p.A.

Picture acknowledgements
The publishers gratefully acknowledge the permission of the following to use their photographs in this book: John Frost 19; Image Select/Archiv für Kunst und Geschichte 5, 8, 9, 13, 15, 22, 32, 33, 38, 43; Imperial War Museum 12, 14, 21, 41, 42 both; Lord's Gallery 31 top; National Cartoon Archive 26; National Film Archive 39, 40; Popperfoto 4, 11, 16, 18, 24, 31 bottom, 34, 35; Punch 25; Wayland Picture Library 6, 7, 10, 20, 23, 28, 29, 30, 36.

Contents

An English version of a Soviet anti-Nazi propaganda poster, showing Hitler eating the bones of the people of Europe.

Domestic propaganda worked only if governments kept a firm control over all information and views being given to the people. This was easy as far as official announcements were concerned, for they came directly from the governments themselves. To control other information, governments used censorship. In the totalitarian states (Germany, Italy and the USSR) and Japan, this was often heavy-handed. In the democracies the approach was more subtle. The media was left to censor itself according to official guidelines, the government stepping in only when the system broke down. (For a discussion of censorship see chapter 5). Nevertheless, on both sides the effect was the same: the appearance of material which might harm the war effort was strictly prohibited. Bad news was not automatically ruled out: the bombing of a city, for example, could be used to show how wicked the enemy was in killing defenceless civilians. It might be argued, therefore, that during the war everything produced by the media was propaganda.

Spreading propaganda was a tricky business. Sometimes it could 'boomerang' (see panel on opposite page). If its claims were too exaggerated, then people no longer believed them. In the open societies of the West the morality of propaganda, especially black propaganda, was often questioned by those who knew of its existence. The Americans were particularly worried. President Roosevelt told his people that they were fighting for '*four essential human freedoms*', one of which was the freedom of speech and expression. Some people asked how America could fight for freedom of expression by using censorship and lies, the very evils it was supposed to be fighting against. '*Democracy itself seemed endangered*' by the battle to preserve it. (Allan M. Winkler, *The Politics of Propaganda*.)

Every possible means was used to get propaganda across. These included radio broadcasts, public speeches and meetings, posters, films, cartoons, leaflets, newspapers, songs, stage shows, and even

your **BRITAIN** · *fight for it* ***now***

FRANK NEWBOULD

ISSUED BY A·B·C·A

spreading rumours and getting support from religious organizations. Some propaganda came directly from the government; other propaganda was produced by individuals not directly under government control, such as actors and journalists. At the time it was considered vital to the war effort and took up an immense amount of time, money and effort. However, as you read the pages which follow, you might ask yourself whether it was all worth it. What influence, if any, did propaganda have on the outcome of the war?

Badly-thought-out British propaganda? Since the majority of the nation lived in industrial towns, the country shown in the picture was not what most people were fighting for.

Propaganda boomerangs

Untrue claims and mistakes were known as propaganda boomerangs. In mid-1940, German propaganda minister Goebbels announced that there was a *'feeling of panic'* in Britain and the country would soon fall to the Nazis. When this proved to be untrue his propaganda machine was discredited. Early US anti-Japanese propaganda was spoilt by lack of attention to detail: some pictures showed kimonos worn the wrong way, for example. Similarly, poor translation sometimes made Japanese propaganda more of a joke than a threat. Who could take seriously the remark: *'Japanese men look furious, but they are sweet inside'*? (Anthony Rhodes, *Propaganda.*)

7

Government organizations

Every government fighting the Second World War used propaganda. This was partly because it was widely believed that propaganda had played a major part in the First World War, particularly in undermining German morale in 1918. Governments also gave propaganda a good deal of attention simply because they had to: once one country had entered the war of words (and the German and Italian fascists were using massive propaganda even before they came to power), other nations were obliged to counteract enemy propaganda with material of their own. Even the Japanese, who had considered propaganda contrary to '*the true spirit of Japanese knighthood*', soon adopted methods pioneered in the West.
(Anthony Rhodes, *Propaganda*.)

Finally, it was generally recognized that in a war that affected every member of the nations taking part, not just the armed forces, morale of civilians was just as important as that of the armed forces.

General Erich Ludendorff, a German general in the First World War. (See box on right.)

Propaganda and the German defeat, 1918

In 1919 the German general Ludendorff claimed that, '*we were hypnotised by the enemy propaganda as a rabbit by a snake. It was exceptionally clever and on a grand scale.*' (*War Memoirs*.) This claim has since been questioned by historians and is now seen as clever propaganda in its own right. It helped to build up the idea – adopted by the Nazis – that the German army had been 'stabbed in the back' by politicians who had been persuaded to surrender while the army was still fighting.

Josef Paul Goebbels (1897-1945)
A brilliant public speaker and highly intelligent master of the techniques of mass communication, Goebbels was responsible for selling the Third Reich to the German people and the wider world. On the outbreak of war he lost influence and had difficulty in combatting the influence of Reich press chief Otto Dietrich and the army's own Propaganda Section. To win back his position and ensure full popular backing for the Nazis' struggle, from 1943 he pushed the propaganda concepts of a war that everyone, not just soldiers, was part of, and the fight to the death. When Germany was defeated he poisoned his family and shot himself.

The first and best-known propaganda ministry during the era of the Second World War was the German Reich Ministry for Public Enlightenment and Propaganda, headed from 13 March 1933 by Josef Paul Goebbels. In theory the ministry had complete control over all legally-distributed information, although in practice the administration of the Third Reich was not as efficient as some observers believed. Personal rivalry between Goebbels and other leaders sometimes led to policy conflicts. Using the Press Law of 1933 Goebbels told editors exactly which news to print and closed down newspapers which would not do as he demanded (such as the *Vossische Zeitung*, which had been published since 1704). He even told editors which headlines to use. Similarly, the Reich Broadcasting Company came under his control. Before the war, films and other cultural output remained largely in private hands, although the Reich Chambers of Films and Culture permitted only material that supported the Nazi view of the state. One exception was official *Staatsauftragsfilms*, so boring that audiences often hissed during performances.

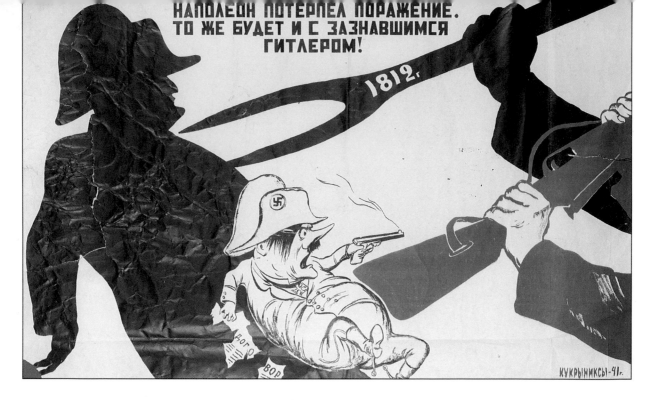

НАПОЛЕОН ПОТЕРПЕЛ ПОРАЖЕНИЕ.
ТО ЖЕ БУДЕТ И С ЗАЗНАВШИМСЯ
ГИТЛЕРОМ!

1812,

КУКРЫНИКСЫ-41г.

A Soviet poster suggesting that the Red Army would drive back Hitler as the Russians had driven back Napoleon in 1812. What do you think the USSR's Free French allies thought of the suggestion?

British propaganda was co-ordinated by the Ministry of Information (MoI), opened in September 1939. From August 1941 the MoI was helped by a special Political Warfare Executive (PWE), responsible for (mostly black) propaganda aimed at other countries. Theoretically these organizations had total power over all information, whether in words, pictures or on film. The MoI issued posters, leaflets, documentary films and books (such as the successful account of the Blitz: *Front Line, 1940-41*). The British government relied more heavily than the Germans on the independent support of people such as newspaper editors.

In 1939 the USA was the only major power lacking an official propaganda agency. By August 1940 President Roosevelt had taken steps to rectify this by creating the Office of Government Reports (OGR) and the Co-ordinator of Inter-American Affairs (CIAA), which concerned themselves with putting out accurate information about the US defence programme. A year later, as war became more likely for the US, Roosevelt reorganized his country's propaganda machinery by abolishing the CIAA and setting up the Office of the Co-ordinator of Information (OCI), which became the

Office of Strategic Services (OSS) in 1942. The OSS supervised intelligence gathering and propaganda to enemy and neutral countries. It built up a worldwide staff of 12,000 and its large-scale disinformation (black propaganda) radio campaigns were just as unscrupulous as anything used by America's enemies. US domestic propaganda was under the control of the Office of War Information. Probably the most powerful US propaganda came from the Hollywood film studios, which from mid-1941 voluntarily made movies intended to help the Allied cause. (See chapter 7.)

When the USA entered the war after the Japanese attack on Pearl Harbor, it became necessary for the Allies to co-ordinate their propaganda efforts. This was done by integrating the work of the OSS with the British Special Operations Executive (SOE) and by setting up a Psychological Warfare Division of the Supreme Headquarters Allied Expeditionary Force. The Axis powers possessed no comparable organization.

William J Donovan (1883-1959)
A veteran of World War I and personal friend of President Roosevelt, Donovan headed the OCI (which he had asked the president to set up) and OSS. He believed that propaganda was 'an attack weapon . . . the arrow of initial penetration' and used a subtle blend of rumour and lies in an attempt to undermine the morale of the USA's enemies. His highly-independent OSS was mistrusted by politicians and generals, and disbanded in October 1945.

A US government poster to increase workers' participation in the war. It combines Nazi swastika and Japanese sun.

Radio Tokyo

Radio Tokyo was the most important of several stations controlled by the NHK. From 1942 it was a major propaganda organ, directing broadcasts at the USA (see pages 36–37) and the peoples of countries occupied by the Japanese. By 1944, as the prospect of defeat loomed, it concentrated less on attacking Japan's enemies and more on keeping up morale at home with cultural and light entertainment programmes. As US bombers began to pound the Japanese mainland the NHK set up an air-raid warning service.

Britain and the USA were never able to co-operate with their Soviet allies over propaganda. When the USSR joined the war in 1941 there was no need to establish any new organs of propaganda: the Communist Party had always controlled the Soviet media and exercised a strict control over the arts. Some twenty years previously all printing and paper supply had been put into the hands of the State Publicity Corporation. This had its own censorship department which concerned itself even with maps. The Political Education Committee, with branches all over the USSR, made sure that everyone knew the party line. The secret police, the NKVD, were quick to stamp out any signs of dissent. All that was needed once war had begun was to reinforce the cult of the leader, Stalin, (see chapter 6) and aim negative propaganda at the fascists. The Russian Orthodox Church was more favourably regarded (see chapter 5) and the hatred previously heaped on all capitalist countries was aimed at the USSR's enemies. An interesting result of the need for wartime propaganda was that democratic countries such as Britain and the USA, which had previously criticized the Soviet Union's use of censorship and propaganda, now found themselves employing precisely the same devices.

Japan had no single propaganda minister. Nevertheless, as early as 1932 the Education Ministry had set up a Bureau of Thought Supervision. There was also careful censorship, and the Communications Ministry ensured that the government line was effectively put across to the domestic population, neutral countries and enemies. From 1942 a Cabinet Information Board was established to co-ordinate control of all press and radio output. The country's most powerful propaganda weapon was the Japanese Broadcasting Association (NHK), which had been given a monopoly of radio broadcasting and put under Communications Ministry control in 1926. The army also had its own broadcasting service, which broadcast factual information for soldiers.

Official propaganda 1: 'Tell big lies'

Official or 'national' propaganda directly controlled by the government and aimed at its own citizens had two aims. (1) To help its own cause by raising morale and justifying the cause for which its people were fighting, and (2) to put down the enemy. Of course the two often overlapped. For example, the Japanese broadcasts announcing the capture of Singapore by Japanese armies used the opportunity both to praise Japanese military strength and mock that of the British. In America official propaganda, especially if it carried a picture of President Roosevelt, sometimes aroused great hostility among his political opponents. Unlike Britain, the USA did not cancel elections during wartime; some people felt that government war propaganda helped Roosevelt to be re-elected president in 1944.

Hitler at a Nazi rally, 1934. The Führer (leader) disliked broadcasting on radio, much preferring the more direct, emotional appeal of the public meeting.

Winston Churchill's style was very distinctive: a 'Victory' sign, cigar and look of dogged resistance.

Propaganda put out by governments generally had one of three targets: one's own side, the enemy and neutrals. Some propaganda tried to persuade neutrals either to join the side of the propagandist, or at least to look favourably on it. One piece of propaganda might take in more than one target. Some of the best-known examples of this device were the speeches that Churchill delivered in 1940-41 (see box), trying to get the USA to join the war.

One of the simplest propaganda techniques was a personal appearance by a war leader. This might take the form of a relatively low-key visit to a war zone, as when Churchill wandered through the ruins of bombed London, chatting to people and providing excellent opportunities for morale-raising photographs in the newspapers.

More dramatic were political rallies, when leaders appeared on a platform and addressed massive crowds of troops and citizens. Before the outbreak of war Hitler used this tactic to great effect. He deliberately kept his audience waiting, so that they were overjoyed at his eventual appearance. Then he stirred them to a frenzy with rousing speeches in which he told people what they wanted to hear rather than actual facts. His central propaganda idea was, '*When you tell lies, tell big lies*'. The Japanese also went in for massive political rallies, sometimes coinciding with Patriotic Weeks, such as the Anti-Espionage Week.

During the war Hitler's public appearances became fewer and fewer, and after the Stalingrad defeat of 1942-3 he made only three public speeches. The main weakness of personal appearances as a propaganda technique was that they reached only a comparatively few people. Although they could be filmed and shown to millions, it was difficult to recapture the excitement of the original gathering. And Hitler did not perform well on the radio. (For more on the cult of the leader, see chapter 6.)

Both Britain and Germany experimented with television broadcasts in the 1930s, but the medium was

ВПЕРЕД, ЗА РАЗГРОМ НЕМЕЦКИХ ЗАХВАТЧИКОВ И ИЗГНАНИЕ ИХ ИЗ ПРЕДЕЛОВ НАШЕЙ РОДИНЫ!

Stalin points the way for the Soviet forces to burst through into Germany, 1944. There was scarcely an item of Soviet propaganda that did not somehow involve Stalin.

not properly developed until after the war. As a result, during the period 1939-45, radio broadcasting was the main way to reach the public. Radio crossed frontiers and entered every home equipped with a radio set. This made it the most important of all propaganda weapons available.

Non-government radio stations existed in all countries. The extent to which they were used for government propaganda varied a good deal. In Britain and America, where the transmitters were owned by independent organizations, governments could

Independent domestic broadcasting

The decision of the democratic states to entrust most radio broadcasting to non-government stations can be interpreted in three ways. Either they were so confident of people's support that they did not feel it necessary to do more than keep a watchful eye over radio output; or they were not powerful enough to exercise total control over the media; or leaving broadcasting services in independent hands was in itself a subtle piece of propaganda: it told the world that they believed in the freedom of speech. Nevertheless, no country, however independent its radio, was allowed broadcasting that undermined the government's view.

use radio broadcasts for public announcements and major political speeches. Otherwise they allowed programmers a comparatively free hand, within the limits of censorship. (For more on the role of the BBC during the war, see chapter 7.)

In Germany and Japan there was more direct government interference, although it was found that if broadcasts were too obviously biased or dull, listeners just switched off. With this in mind, the Japanese authorities tried to keep audiences' spirits up with popular programmes, mixed in with campaigns which warned, for example, that surrender to the Americans would mean prostitution and castration for the Japanese people by 'redheaded barbarians from the West'. (Anthony Rhodes, *Propaganda*.) Towards the end of the war, as the situation became desperate, Japanese radio even invented famous victories in a pitiful attempt to keep up morale. Soviet radio was also heavily government-controlled. The Soviet people accepted this partly because they had never known anything else.

A British family, gas masks at the ready, tune in to the BBC news in 1938. After 1939, during the war the BBC's one domestic channel operated a system of self-censorship. Radio was listened to by many people during the war, and so was an important vehicle for propaganda. Pictures such as this made effective propaganda, because they showed that everyone was involved in the war, not just the fighting forces.

Long propaganda pamphlets and books were produced for domestic consumption. Hitler's *Mein Kampf*, in which he set out, among other matters, his racist ideas on German superiority and his hatred for Jewish people, had sold six million copies by 1940 and continued to be printed and sold for the rest of the war. Ironically, extracts from it were printed in one of the American OWI's many publications, *Negroes and the War*. This sought to explain to black Americans that they should support the war because, although they had suffered discrimination in the USA, America had '*come a long way in the last fifty years*' and they could expect no sympathy from the racist Nazis. The British MoI also produced a steady stream of publications. Some, such as *Wartime Recipies*, issued in conjunction with the Ministry of Food, were intended to make wartime restrictions less unattractive. Others, like *The Battle of Britain and the Front Line, 1940-41*, praised the bravery and morale of ordinary citizens.

Posters were another popular official propaganda medium. When well used they were a good way of getting over the government's message, but if wrongly handled they could turn out to be disastrous boomerangs. (See page 7.) The best posters carried a simple, memorable slogan and striking illustration, often in cartoon form. The British in particular also employed humour. A picture could create an instant image of a villainous enemy and contrast it with a more favourable view of one's own side. Some posters were used as part of educational campaigns. Kenneth Bird (known as *Fougasse*), for example, drew a fine series of posters to support the MoI's 'Careless talk Costs Lives' campaign, warning of the dangers of spreading information which might be used by the enemy. The equivalent German campaign went under the title 'The Enemy is Listening', while the Japanese used monkeys who could 'Hear no Evil, See no Evil, Speak no Evil'. Posters could also make a general point, such as a Russian one which showed a feeble Hitler being strangled by the Allies.

A British poster shows the effects of a German bombing raid on the town of Scarborough. The poster aimed to encourage men to join the armed forces so that they could protect their homes and families.

A 1942 US poster warning that talking about military matters in public could help the enemy, and result in needless deaths.

British Army propaganda: the Army Film Unit making The People's Army, *a movie intended to improve relations between the army and the civilian population.*

Before the age of television, the cinema was extremely popular and governments were quick to realize its potential as a propaganda weapon. Cinemas generally showed at least three films in a programme, often including a newsreel and a documentary. All governments used these types of film for propaganda. Goebbels' ministry sometimes put several German newsreels together to make full-length documentaries, such as *Feuertaufe* about the conquest of Poland. In America the OWI produced a series of documentaries with rather dull titles like *Fuel Conservation, Salvage* and *Doctors at War.*

More interesting, and more subtle in their propaganda effect, were full-length feature films, but only in the USSR were these entirely in the hands of the state. (See chapters 5 and 7.) In Germany the government told studios how many political or entertainment films they were to make.

The Japanese came up with films on all sorts of subjects, ranging from the rather obvious *The Last Days of the British Empire* to *A Record of Love*, which encouraged Japanese women to marry injured servicemen.

Although they were not afraid to use the censor's scissors, democratic governments felt it was better not to get too closely involved in feature films: it was thought that as long as they kept people happy, such films helped to keep up morale.

In schools every wartime government had a captive audience for its propaganda. Children were taught that their side was fighting for justice, freedom and truth. In the totalitarian states this was reinforced with specially-written text books which in Germany gave the Nazi, or in the USSR communist, view of a subject. In both these countries pupils were encouraged to report unpatriotic teachers to the authorities. Italian schoolchildren were told that, *'A book and a rifle make a perfect Fascist'*. (Anthony Rhodes, *Propaganda*.) The Japanese education service came totally under army control with the appointment of an army officer as Minister of Education in 1935. Military training joined the school curriculum, the day began with a flag-saluting ceremony and every month a Morning Address was broadcast to schools on topics such as *'Why Our Military Forces Are Strong'*.

Finally there were government-inspired rumour campaigns. Since accurate information was always very difficult to get hold of, rumour spread rapidly. A good example of the official use of this 'mouth propaganda' came in the spring of 1941, when Hitler was preparing to attack the Soviet Union. Since it was impossible to hide the build-up of troops on the eastern front, the German High Command put out the rumour that they were really going to invade England. The troops in the east, they suggested, were there to trick the English – *'the greatest undertaking in deception in the history of warfare'*. (Jay W. Baird, *The Mythical World of Nazi War Propaganda*.)

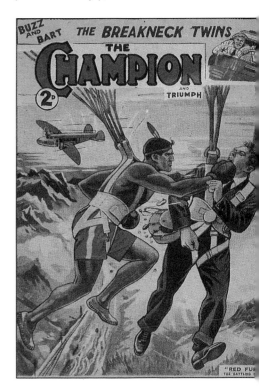

Propaganda for children: comic hero Red Fury tackles a German parachute spy, 1941.

Official propaganda 2: 'Heil Himmler!'

During the war millions of leaflets and other documents were dropped by plane over enemy territory. Most were Allied products, as for most of the war they had air superiority. Some were white propaganda, others were black; great care was taken to make the latter appear genuine. The best leaflet campaigns were well co-ordinated with military action, like those used by the Americans on Japan in 1945. From Pearl Harbor (Dec, 1941) to 1 May 1945 the USA dropped 90,000,000 leaflets over the Far East. Over the next three months a further 98,000,000 rained down on Japan alone. Some set out the Allied peace terms promising that Japan would not be enslaved; others

William Joyce, whose upper-class accent led to him being known as Lord Haw Haw. Joyce was an English Nazi who went to Germany to make propaganda broadcasts aimed at Britain. At the end of the war he was captured and executed as a traitor, which shows how seriously his broadcasts must have been taken.

named the cities which were to be bombed, asking civilians to evacuate them. At the war's end, leaflets told of the attack on Hiroshima and informed the Japanese people that their government had made a peace offer when this move had not been made public.

Radio broadcasts to other countries varied between the comparatively accurate transmissions of the BBC and the Voice of America, which told of defeats as well as victories, to the many black services beamed at enemy territory by all states that could afford them. Throughout Europe the BBC was widely respected, both in neutral countries and those occupied by the Nazis; even Germans tuned in to get a reasonably balanced account of what was going on (as well as good light music). This so annoyed Goebbels that he banned listening to all foreign radio stations. Towards the end of the war the Japanese similarly forbade listening to foreign broadcasts. The British and American governments never issued such orders. This decision was said to have been made in the name of freedom, but it stemmed as much from the fact that the bans were impossible to police.

Bomb damage in Norwich, 1940. Dreadful events such as this could be used to make people want to fight the enemy.

Black leaflets

The Allies dropped a huge range of black propaganda on Germany. It included notices which read 'Heil Himmler!' (suggesting that Himmler was trying to become Führer), forged banknotes, postage stamps, ration cards and blank leave passes for German troops. One particularly subtle move was to print editions of the German army newspaper, *Nachrichten für die Truppe*. These were filled with such exaggerated reports of the weakness of the Allied armies that readers were led to question the paper's honesty.

This 1936 poster urges Germans to tune in to the radio, but they were banned from listening to foreign stations in case they heard anti-Nazi propaganda.

German 'white' broadcasts (eg Radio Hamburg, beamed at England) were also quite successful, particularly in the early years of the war. Some British listeners found Radio Hamburg's news and comment more interesting than the bald facts given by the BBC. During air raids, when some domestic transmitters were shut down to avoid helping enemy bombers, German radio could be more clearly received than English radio broadcasts. The same applied in Germany during periods of heavy Allied air attack. The white Soviet broadcasts to Germany were a great success story. In the winter of 1943-4 it was found that the Soviet broadcasts were more popular than their Allied counterparts, perhaps because the USSR was not bombing German cities and their propaganda made much of a basic friendship between the ordinary citizens of the two countries.

Most black broadcasts pretended to come from within the country they were aimed at but were in fact produced abroad. Truth was the least of their concerns – the British government was shocked by the stories about Germany that British stations used to attract listeners. Among the black radio stations were the British GS1, which spoke to Germany and occupied Europe, the Russian National Committee for Free Germany (broadcast from the USSR), Germany's New British Broadcasting Station and Christian Peace Movement, and the numerous American stations operated in the Pacific by the OSS. It is impossible to tell how effective the broadcasts of these stations were. Listeners were confused, annoyed, amused and, perhaps, persuaded by black radio broadcasts that were aimed at them. We know that GS1 had huge audiences, but we do not know how seriously its message was taken. Foreign broadcasts could be countered by jamming, forbidding people to listen to them, or by preparing counter-broadcasts. For example, after Lord Haw-Haw's programmes (see page 20), the BBC employed the writer JB Priestley to reply with a reassuring commentary of his own.

The people speak: 'A good laugh'

During the war (as in peacetime) most people had a fairly cynical attitude towards government. They were often suspicious of official propaganda – as with some of the early British MoI posters. They were often more ready to accept propaganda when it was presented unofficially, perhaps in a song, a feature film made by a private film company, from their local church or even in a newspaper which was not controlled directly by the government. All governments recognized this, but felt the need to exercise control over what was put before the public. Governments controlled information through censorship.

The USSR and Britain make an interesting comparison of the way governments approached censorship. Soviet censorship was the most comprehensive of any of the major war powers. In the USSR everyone in a position of influence was expected to be a member of the Communist Party and all material had to have prior Party approval. If anything – a film, a broadcast, a newspaper article or even a cartoon – appeared which went against the Party line, its creator was likely to lose his or her post and end up in prison or a labour camp. Shostakovich, an internationally famous composer, was expected to produce patriotic, morale-raising music: his Seventh Symphony, composed during the 890-day long German siege of Leningrad (now St Petersburg), met with official approval because it depicted peace, struggle and eventual Soviet victory.

British censorship seemed to operate differently.

Why do you think this 1943 Soviet poster shows the enemy as a lion, rather than as a weaker creature?

The censor
A [government] official who examines books, papers, telegrams, letters, films, etc., with powers to delete material, or to forbid publication, delivery, or showing.

23

Only material that was going to be sent abroad had to be shown to a censor in advance; otherwise people were free to say what they wanted, but under Defence Regulation 3 they were liable to prosecution for putting forward information which might be of 'military value' to the enemy. The nature of this information was not very clearly set out in *Defence Notices*. As a consequence of *Defence Notices* not being clear, men and women working in the media preferred to submit doubtful pieces to the government in advance, rather than be prosecuted later.

'*The censorship system was thus based on bluff, goodwill (for no editor wanted to help the Germans) and the realisation that, if it broke down, a . . . compulsory scheme would have to be substituted.*' (Michael Balfour, *Propaganda in War 1939-1945*.) Was British censorship very different in its effect from that operating in the USSR? (See panel.)

Generally, the more successful a country was in battle, the less its government was criticized and the more it could rely on the support of unofficial propaganda. As Sir Robert Bruce-Lockhart, the operational head of the British Department

Dimitri Shostakovich, the celebrated Russian composer, was expected to produce work celebrating the Soviet war achievement.

Propaganda by irony: the caption to this 1940 cartoon read, '… meanwhile, in Britain, the entire population, faced by the threat of invasion, has been flung into a state of complete panic …'

of Propaganda, observed: '*Propaganda is, or should be, easy for the winning side, and difficult for the losing side.*' *(Comes the Reckoning.)* Certainly, the British government's attacks on the press came in the first half of the war, when things were going badly for the Allies. As the invasion of the USSR began to go badly over the winter of 1941-2, the independent German film industry was brought under more direct government control. Radio Tokyo was subject to tighter and tighter controls as the Americans slowly fought their way across the Pacific to Japan. Does this tell us something about the power of propaganda? Perhaps propaganda reflected rather than influenced the way people felt about the war?

The power of cartoons published in independent newspapers is well illustrated by the example above, which was printed in *Punch* on 14 August 1940. The message is subtle. The caption, supposed to be German propaganda, is contradicted by the attitude of the men in the pub. The drawing was considered so effective that the MoI reprinted it in propaganda leaflets sent to British colonies. What do you think its message is? Why do you think that some members of the British public felt that '*A good laugh kept you going better than anything else*'?

Cartoons from independent artists could also be critical of the government. The Zec drawing in the *Daily Mirror* of 6 March 1942 (below) can be seen in two ways. Either it is praising the sailors who struggle to maintain British petrol supplies and asks people to use fuel sparingly; or it is being critical of the profits of the petrol companies and, perhaps, calling for peace. Winston Churchill took the latter view. He called the cartoon 'defeatist' and considered shutting down the *Daily Mirror*. What do you think the cartoon is saying?

In all countries stars of popular entertainment were expected to use their talents to help in the war effort, but only in the democratic countries were they free to put on their own shows and programmes. London's Windmill Theatre, famous for its '*We Never Close*' motto, seemed to symbolize British resistance.

Critical or complimentary? This British cartoon's controversial caption read '"The price of petrol has been increased by one penny." Official.' Churchill thought it critical, and considered trying to shut the newspaper that printed it.

Vera Lynn entertains British troops during the war: she was so popular that she became known as the Forces' Sweetheart. Many governments paid for popular entertainers to visit troops, because it was felt that this made the fighting forces feel happier about being in the war away from their families.

The BBC's light entertainment division, featuring songs such as 'We'll Meet Again' and 'The White Cliffs of Dover' from the *'Forces' Sweetheart'* Vera Lynn, played a major part in keeping people happy. (For more on the BBC see chapter 7.) Although not as obviously propagandist as official posters and films, songs which set out to raise flagging spirits obviously played a part in the battle for people's hearts and minds, and must therefore be seen as propaganda. It is no surprise that governments were prepared to pay for popular performers to give live performances to the troops at the front.

After Pearl Harbor the mighty US entertainment business joined the propaganda war with a new wave of shows, films (see chapter 7), songs and broadcasts. The titles of some of the more obviously propagandist songs give an idea of their blunt, patriotic message: 'Remember Pearl Harbor', 'Der Führer's Face', 'There'll be no Adolf Hitler nor Yellow Japs to Fear', 'We're Gonna Have to Slap the Dirty Little Jap' and 'Praise the Lord and Pass the Ammunition'. Englishman Noel Coward's 'Don't Let's be Beastly to the Germans' had a more tongue-in-cheek approach to the same patriotic theme.

Walt Disney's war
Here are some of the words of the 1942 Oliver Wallace song 'Der Führer's Face', which featured in a Walt Disney Donald Duck cartoon film of the same title:
Ven der Führer says, 'Ve iss der masder race,'
Ve Heil! Heil! Right in Der Führer's face,
Not to luff der Führer is a great disgrace,
Ve Heil! Heil! Right in Der Führer's Face.
Iss ve not der Supermen?
Aryan pure, supermen?
Ya! Ve iss der Supermen,
Super, Duper, Supermen!

All governments sought to use religion for propaganda purposes. Even Stalin's USSR, officially an atheist state (which meant it had opposed all religion) relaxed its attitude during the war in order to get religious support. Ministers understood that the faithful were more likely to believe the words of a priest than those of a politician.

Religion and politics were most closely connected in Japan. The country was believed to be a divine land, its people more spiritual than others and its emperor directly descended from the sun god.

Propaganda in Japan was built on the idea of the country being destined to rule the Pacific, and persuaded its people to endure tremendous hardships (even undertaking suicide missions) in the belief that they could never be defeated.

In the West, religion was less used as a propaganda weapon. Priests were attached to all units and offered counselling to the troops. Archbishop William Temple, head of the Church of England, believed, '*that the War had to be fought and had to be won. War was the lesser of two evils . . .* [and] *its use could offset the forces of evil.*' (Edward Carpenter, *Cantuar.*) Nevertheless, the Bible asks Christians to 'turn the other cheek' to aggressors so some were unhappy to be at war. The BBC's religious broadcasts to Germany kept

Much Japanese propaganda reminded the Japanese people – and especially soldiers – of their Samurai warrior past.

THIS IS THE ENEMY

American anti-Nazi propaganda. Both Allied and Axis countries claimed to have God on their side: this poster shows the Nazis attacking Christianity and therefore suggests that America was defending it. How do you think non-Christians would have felt about this message?

largely out of politics. The French radio station Radio Catholique, the broadcasts of which were aimed at parish priests, accepted that the priests themselves might not want to get involved in resistance activities. The poster above, which is American, is one of the few examples of propaganda that was obviously anti-Nazi and pro-Christian. What is its message? How do you think a non-Christian might have reacted to it?

The cult of the leader: 'The great one from above'

A Soviet cartoon life-story of Adolf Hitler, aimed at making him seem ridiculous.

For best effect, domestic propaganda needed a focus. This focus could be an unspecific one, such as victory or the fatherland. In all countries there was a tendency to build up the image of the national leader as a figure behind whom people could unite. Individuals are easier to get widespread support for than ideas. We see this illustrated in elections nowadays, when more attention is often given to the personality of a party's leader than to the policies that the party will practice.

Japan had always laid heavy stress on the semi-divine emperor, even in peacetime. Before the outbreak of war the dictators of totalitarian states, notably Hitler, Mussolini and Stalin, also became the centres of personality cults. A significant wartime development was the way the leaders of democratic states were similarly treated. Roosevelt and Churchill became symbols of their countries' cause in a manner which would have been impossible in peacetime.

The first personality cult of the era of the Second World War was based around the Italian fascist dictator Benito Mussolini, who came to power in 1922. Mussolini associated himself with every aspect of Italian life. Italian propaganda produced some brilliant slogans and posters, but was never as well organized as its German or Soviet counterparts, and an Italian Propaganda Ministry was set up only in 1937.

Mussolini, who had been a journalist and understood the power of the media, made sure that he was always portrayed as the heart of Italian fascism. His picture appeared everywhere. He made showy, dramatic appearances, sometimes speaking to excited crowds from the balcony of the Palazzo Venezia in Rome (being a short man he always made sure he stood above those around him) and sometimes, stripped to the waist, joining workers in a grand engineering or agricultural project. The Italian people were bombarded with slogans, such as, '*Caesar has come to life again in the Duce* [leader]' or '*Mussolini is always right.*' This was all very well when things were going well for the Italians. But when their armies suffered defeat after defeat the idea that Mussolini was always right began to sound ridiculous, which also made Mussolini seem ridiculous.

The Italian leader, Mussolini, photographed visiting the new Fiat motor car factory in Turin, during 1939. Mussolini thought that public appearances were good propaganda material, and was always keen to make them.

The cult of the leader was perfected in Germany, although it was strongest in the USSR. In Germany the Nazi propaganda machine successfully put over the image of Hitler as '*the great one from above*' who had come to save his people and make them great again.

This image of Hitler was carefully created. Not one word of criticism of him was ever allowed to be legally written, spoken or printed. Countless pictures and posters showed him in all the roles expected of a leader: stern, determined, thoughtful and caring (he was often photographed with children). He was shown as concerned for all sections of German society, from factory workers to army officers. He was given credit for all his country's successes and others were blamed if things went wrong. There were songs, films, plays, books and poems about him, all exalting his virtues. As the popular slogan said, he **was** the Third Reich: *Ein Volk, Ein Reich, Ein Führer* (One People, One Realm, One Führer). Perhaps it is a measure of the success of the Hitler cult that when the 1944 slogan *Hitler is Victory* had been shown to be patently untrue and Allied forces were advancing on Berlin, some Germans were prepared to fight on in the belief that somehow their Führer would save them. In the end only Hitler's suicide broke the spell he had cast.

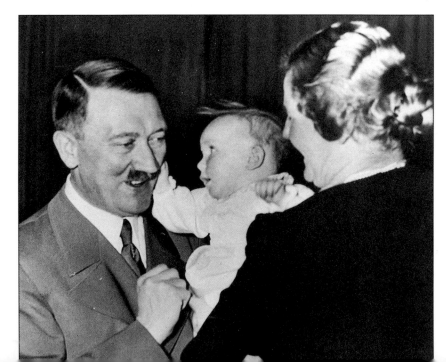

The war leader with a soft heart. The picture was taken to show that Hitler could be as kindly towards Germans as he was ruthless towards the country's enemies. Even babies loved him!

ДУХ ВЕЛИКОГО ЛЕНИНА И ЕГО ПОБЕДОНОСНОЕ ЗНАМЯ ВДОХНОВЛЯЮТ НАС ТЕПЕРЬ НА ОТЕЧЕСТВЕННУЮ ВОЙНУ... (И. Сталин)

The poster above shows a common theme in Soviet propaganda. It implies that Stalin was the natural and approved successor to Lenin (in the background), the founder of the USSR. In fact, Stalin was not Lenin's choice for the next leader of the Soviet Union.

The Churchill personality cult was not built up as deliberately as those of Hitler or Mussolini, but in some ways it proved almost as powerful. This was partly Churchill's own doing. Despite admitting to only a passing regard for the importance of propaganda, once saying '*This is a war of deeds, not words!*' (Anthony Rhodes, *Propaganda*), in public he was careful to adopt a considered pose: grim-faced, cigar-chewing, dogged, reliable and always giving the V for Victory sign – the British Bulldog. This could be easily portrayed by cartoonists. He alone addressed the nation at crucial moments during the war and his form was shown on propaganda posters at home and abroad.

Churchill was certainly an actor. It may be that he recognized the British need for an inspiring war leader and enjoyed playing the part with great skill. Propaganda supported his image, but probably did not create it. In the election of 1945, when the war was over, Churchill was rejected as a peacetime prime minister, suggesting that wartime propaganda's effect did not help a politician once peace was declared.

Case studies

'It's That Man Again'

During the war, relations between the BBC and the government were not always easy. The BBC was funded by licence fees that were supposed to be paid by everyone who owned a radio set. Defence Regulations gave the government the authority to control what the BBC broadcast. On several occasions MPs called for these powers to be used to oversee the BBC's domestic service more closely. (Its role as a transmitter of propaganda abroad was never questioned.) In practice, however, the BBC's British broadcasts maintained a semi-independent position. The BBC stuck to a distinction between propaganda (*'the perversion of public opinion'*, as the Controller of Programmes put it), which it would not engage in, and what it called *'executive information'*, or accurate news about recent events. (Michael Balfour, *Propaganda in War.*)

The cast of ITMA – It's That Man Again – the British radio comedy show which amused people by poking fun at government institutions such as the 'Ministry of Twerps' (the Ministry of Works).

Tommy Handley (centre), star of ITMA, with Lind Joyce and Michele de Lys. Handley's humour kept the whole wartime generation laughing.

Ironically, the BBC's most effective domestic propaganda came neither from news programmes nor even, in the later stages of the war, from the speeches of the prime minister. It was provided by a light entertainment comedy programme, 'It's That Man Again' or ITMA: the *'classic programme of the war'*. (Asa Briggs, *The War of Words*.)

ITMA was nonsense comedy in the style which Monty Python made popular on TV years later. In it nothing was sacred, and it was prepared to poke fun at British institutions as much as German. The Ministry of Information, for example, became the Ministry of Aggravation and Mysteries, and the Ministry of Twerps was a clear dig at the Ministry of Works. The show's characters – Colonel Chinstrap, Mona Lot, Mrs Mopp and others – became national institutions. Its catch-phrases, such as *'Boss, boss, something terrible's happened!'*; *'TTFN'* (*TTFN stands for Ta-ta for now*); *'Can I do you now Sir?'*; *'I don't mind if I do'* and *'I'll have to ask me dad'* were on everyone's lips.

Somehow ITMA gave people what they wanted: a chance to relax and laugh at the seriousness which made up so much of their everyday lives during wartime. It can hardly be said to have had a serious point, other than the fact that nothing deserved to be taken too seriously. But that, at the time, was message enough. By bringing a smile to people's lips, ITMA did more for morale than any other single undertaking. It was undoubtedly the most successful British propaganda of the war.

The BBC and propaganda
The BBC agreed with the British Government that the Allies should win the war, and allowed its home service to help in a low-key way. For example, it did not question information provided by the Ministry of Information, even when its correctness appeared doubtful; and in 1942 it set up a Propaganda Unit for domestic broadcasting and introduced more comment into its news programmes. But it never gave up the right to represent a wide range of views, as long as its microphones were not used by *'persons antagonistic to the war effort'*. (Michael Balfour, *Propaganda in War.*)

Broadcasting to the enemy
Radio broadcasts aimed at audiences in enemy countries did not always sound authentic. To be effective they had to show a sound understanding of their audiences' cultural background. One of the best ways to do this was to employ someone who had been brought up in the country to which he or she was broadcasting and spoke the language perfectly. Thus the Germans used Lord Haw-Haw, the Italians the American poet Ezra Pound (captured after the war and confined to a mental institution) and the Japanese broadcast the programmes of Tokyo Rose.

Tokyo Rose

Ms Iva Toguri D'Aquino was a US citizen with Japanese parents. After obtaining a degree in the USA, in 1941 she visited relatives in Japan. Unfortunately for her, war broke out while she was there and she was unable to return to the USA. Recognizing her potential, the Japanese NHK got an American prisoner to train her in broadcasting techniques. Afterwards she and twelve other women began broadcasting propaganda programmes to US troops in the Pacific. Together, these women were known to the troops who listened to them as Tokyo Rose, who they thought was one individual.

Tokyo Rose's technique was to make the troops homesick, so undermining their will to fight. Her broadcasts did this by using accurate first-hand knowledge of the American way of life, playing the conscripted soldiers' favourite swing music and talking sentimentally about the life in America to which they might never return.

US troops fighting on a Pacific island, 1944. Tokyo Rose aimed in her radio broadcasts to make the soldiers feel homesick, and therefore less willing to fight.

Iva Toguri D'Aquino, one of the most successful propaganda broadcasters of the war. She was an American, and therefore able to talk about familiar details of American life in a way that made the soldiers wish they were at home, not fighting in a strange country. After the war she was imprisoned by the US government.

It is not possible to tell precisely how successful Tokyo Rose's broadcasts were, for American morale did not collapse. The very fact that US troops gave her a friendly nickname and tuned in eagerly to her programmes, which they did not consider ridiculous, meant that her message was being listened to. She knew her audience perfectly, and unlike many propagandists she avoided harsh criticism of her enemies and overblown praise of her own side. This enabled her soft propaganda to succeed where a more insensitive approach might have failed.

After the war Ms Toguri D'Aquino was convicted of treason, fined and imprisoned for six years. She claimed, however, that the Japanese had forced her to work for them. Hers was not the only Tokyo Rose voice, and US President Gerald Ford pardoned her in 1977.

Hollywood

By 1939 the US movie industry was by far the largest and most powerful in the world, producing some 650 films each year. Hollywood could have been used as an important propaganda weapon, but for several reasons it was not immediately used as one. Hollywood, the industry's Californian home, had a long tradition of political neutrality. Also, before the USA entered the war, Hollywood films were sold in large numbers in both Germany and Italy. Finally, when war first broke out in Europe, many Americans wanted the USA to stay out of the war and did not want to watch films about it.

By mid-1940, Hollywood's attitude had begun to change. It could no longer sell films to the Axis countries. American Jews, who were financially important to the studios, urged the film makers to take a moral stand against the fate of European Jews. The many British-born actors and directors working in Hollywood, such as Charlie Chaplin, also called for films that encouraged the USA to join the war. By the time the USA went to war itself, Hollywood had prepared the way with a series of anti-Axis movies. No one could mistake the anti-isolationist message of *A Yank in the RAF* (1941) or of *The Great Dictator* (1940), Chaplin's attack on Hitler.

Charlie Chaplin (right) in The Great Dictator, *1940, one of Hollywood's first anti-Nazi movies. Until then the US film industry had tried to sell films to both sides.*

By 1943 three out of every ten Hollywood films were concerned with the war. The new theme suited the studios' style very well, the Nazis or Japanese becoming the 'bad guys' and Allied soldiers, sailors and airmen the 'good guys' who always won in the end. Films such as *Hitler's Children*, *Destination Tokyo*, and *The Story of G.I. Joe* were intended to leave their audiences with little doubt that the war was a straightforward battle between good and evil.

There is no way of measuring the success of the barrage of Hollywood film propaganda, but it must have had some effect on the tens of millions of Americans who were subjected to it in cinemas each week, even if it only reinforced them in their prejudices. Unlike any other government involved in the war, the US administration made relatively few propaganda films of its own. It had no need to: Hollywood did the job instead.

Margaret Lockwood, Rex Harrison and Paul Henreid star in Night Train to Munich *(1940). Once the USA joined the war, Hollywood began to produce large numbers of war movies.*

Evaluation

'Propaganda', wrote the British author Ivor Thomas in 1942, 'is . . . an art, rather than a science; no precise rules can be laid down for successful propaganda, which depends on flair, intuition and inspiration.' (*Warfare by Words.*) This perceptive comment sums up precisely why it is so difficult to estimate the effectiveness of propaganda.

It is impossible to work out why people think the way they do. Why, for example, when both countries had been subjected to similar massive Allied propaganda campaigns, did the Italians lose heart when the war began to go badly, while the Germans

Outside a Berlin cinema showing the Nazi propaganda film, Triumph of Will (Triumph des Willens). Everything, from the lighting to the eagle and flags, was designed to support the film's heroic message.

fought to the bitter end? Might this suggest that propaganda directed towards other countries had little effect on the outcome of the war?

The British historian AJP Taylor scorned the commonly-held idea that, *'Hitler's empire could be shaken by words'*, claiming instead that it, *'could be overthrown only by defeat in the field'*. Taylor claimed that the most valuable thing about British propaganda was that it, *'provided a useful distraction for politically minded Englishmen who might otherwise have been a great nuisance'*! Taylor believed that German propaganda met with *'equally little success'*. (*English History 1914-1945.*)

A less extreme position was taken by Anthony Rhodes. Writing about US propaganda, he decided that, *'propaganda cannot do much against an enemy who is fresh and confident. It is only when defeat sets in that propaganda begins to work.'* But does it? Britain's defeat on the Continent seemed to stiffen its determination to resist Hitler, not weaken it. It was atomic bombs which finally persuaded the Japanese to surrender, not the millions of American leaflets which were dropped on them.

Perhaps propaganda could never change people's thinking, only reinforce it? The Italians, despite Mussolini's propaganda, had never been keen on the war. It was not surprising, therefore, that Italian troops in North Africa were eager to get hold of Allied surrender passes (which guaranteed fair treatment to deserters), even buying them on the black market. The Germans seem to have taken little notice of Allied propaganda; their attitudes tended to change with the military outlook. Seventy-six per cent of German prisoners questioned before the Allied breakthrough during the 1944 Normandy campaign said they supported Hitler. After the breakthrough the figure had fallen to fifty-three per cent.

A straightforward press photograph of victims of a concentration camp – more effective than any official propaganda?

Belief in propaganda

There were always those on both sides who believed that enemy morale was on the verge of collapse, and that effective propaganda could bring it crashing down. One such was the British writer Sebastian Haffner. In *Offensive Against Germany* (1941) he criticized those who said *'Let us only have a few victories. After that propaganda will be easy'*. He claimed that *'Today, victories can no longer be gained unless one's moral armament is as effective as the military and technical armament.'* He concluded with a rousing call: *'England's propaganda offensive against Germany is overdue. Start it NOW.'* There was indeed a massive propaganda offensive against Germany, but the country did not surrender until Allied forces fought their way into Berlin and Hitler killed himself.

A US recruitment poster, 1942.

Which type of propaganda was the most effective? During the war, people believed that leaflets and broadcasting were the best ways of influencing an enemy's thinking. This might well have been so, for they were the only two methods used consistently. Charles Cruickshank's book, *The Fourth Arm*, showed that *'compared with radio, propaganda leaflets counted for very little, and sometimes even did harm'*. It also indicated that Allied white broadcasts to Germany, *'probably had no effect at all'*, while, *'black propaganda probably had more bite in it'*. Since black propaganda often contained lies, what does this suggest about the belief that successful propaganda had to be truthful?

It is even more difficult to say which type of propaganda was most successful in influencing morale at home. The way a people felt was made up of a complicated mix of historical background, culture, economic conditions, confidence in their leaders and how their armed forces were doing: all these made up the mood of a nation at any given moment. Posters, broadcasts, films, newspapers, rallies, education and other propaganda techniques were effective when they were in tune with this mood. It is probably wrong to think that they were ever able to change it.

So did propaganda affect the outcome of the war? Victor Margolin believed that, although it was no substitute for military success, it, *'played an important role in wartime strategy'*. (Foreword to Anthony Rhodes's *Propaganda*.) Michael Balfour was more selective, he thought, *'British propaganda to Germany . . . failed'*, and, *'German*

A US poster calling for help for China, which was also fighting the Japanese. How has the artist tried to make the subject as appealing as possible?

propaganda to Britain had little practical effect', but, 'Britain managed to convince the peoples of Western and Southern Europe that her victory . . . would be in the general interest. The Germans by contrast signally failed to make attractive the system which their victory would have consolidated'. (Propaganda in War.) A similar conclusion might be reached about the US-Japanese propaganda battle.

The last word might be left to Charles Cruickshank: 'it is virtually impossible to assess the part played by propaganda. There is no doubt that it helped [a nation's war effort], but how much can never be said with certainty'. (The Fourth Arm.)

Berlin, 1945. Soviet tank crews celebrate military victory. How much do you think propaganda helped the Allies to win the war? Do you think they would have lost without propaganda?

Successful propaganda

Ivor Thomas listed four ingredients of successful propaganda to enemy countries. It had to be:

1 *'based on policy'* – meaning it should be linked to overall war aims;

2 dependent *'on good intelligence'* – in other words, as we saw with Tokyo Rose, it was convincing when it showed a real understanding of the country to which it was directed;

3 *'linked to strategy'* – Thomas likened propaganda to an artillery bombardment softening up the enemy before an attack;

4 *'truthful – In a long war'*, Thomas wrote, *'deceitful and self-contradictory propaganda would defeat its own object.'* From what you have read, do you think this was so?

Glossary

Absolute ruler   A ruler with complete power.

Allies, the   The USA, Britain and the other countries fighting the Axis powers.

Anti-semitism   Hostility towards the Jewish people.

Armistice   A signed cease-fire.

Aryan   The inaccurate Nazi term for the race of people living in Germany and northern Europe.

Axis   The alliance of Germany, Italy and Japan in the 1930s.

Black market   The illegal buying and selling of goods which are hard to come by in normal shops.

Broadcast   To transmit by radio or television.

Capitalist   The economic system in which the profits of industry go to the owners of the industry.

Civil war   A war fought within a single country.

Communism   A political theory which says that the rewards from an industry should be shared among those who work in it.

Continent, the   Mainland Europe, excluding the British Isles.

Cult   Great admiration among a group for an individual or idea.

D-Day   The code name for the Allied landings on the Normandy beaches, 6 June 1944.

Democracy   Government that ordinary people are able to change if they disagree with it.

Dictatorship   Government by a single, irreplaceable figure, the dictator.

Editor   The person with overall control over the content of a newspaper, film etc.

Fascism   A totalitarian political system laying stress on nationalism and the figure of the leader.

Hiroshima   The Japanese city on which the USA dropped the first atomic bomb on 6 August 1945.

Independence   Freedom from outside control.

Intelligence services   A state's secret information-gathering services.

Isolationism   Not wishing to get involved in foreign affairs.

Jamming   Stopping a radio broadcast being received.

Kimono   A loose Japanese robe.

Labour camp   A prison camp where prisoners were made to work.

Liberal   The political attitude that stresses the rights and freedoms of the individual.

Media   All the means of mass communication – eg radio, TV, newspapers.

Monopoly   Complete control over something. *board game*

Nationalize   Government taking control of an industry.

Neutral   Not taking sides.

Occupy   Take over another territory.

Offensive   An attack.

Patriotism   Love of one's country.

Pearl Harbor The US naval base in Hawaii on which the Japanese launched a surprise air attack on 7 December 1941, thus bringing the USA into the war.

Prosecute Charging someone with a crime in court.

Racism The belief that some human races are 'better' than others, and should be differently treated.

Republic A state without a royal family.

Right wing Opposed to socialism/communism. Fascism is the most extreme right-wing position.

Socialism A political theory which believes that all powerful organizations (businesses etc) should be in the hands of the state.

Third Reich The Nazi empire.

Total war War involving all a country's citizens and industry, not just its armed forces.

Totalitarianism A political system which places all power in the hands of the state and its leader or leaders.

Versailles, Treaty of The treaty imposed on Germany after the First World War in 1918.

Books to read

There are few good books for young readers that deal with or show propaganda. Among them are:

The Home Front Stewart Ross (Wayland, 1990) and *Propaganda* Fiona Reynoldson (Wayland, 1991) both deal specifically with propaganda in Britain during the war. *The Rise of Fascism* Peter Chrisp (Wayland, 1991) contains good examples of propaganda posters and photographs from the Axis powers.

Posters of the Second World War Denis Judd (Wayland, 1972) is now very old, but may still be found in public or school libraries.
The Imperial War Museum in London produces interesting material on many aspects of the era of the Second World War: it is also a fascinating place to visit.

Timeline

1918	11 November	Armistice ends First World War.
1919	28 June	Treaty of Versailles signed.
1922		Mussolini comes to power in Italy
1923-4		Hitler writes *Mein Kampf*.
1926		Japanese radio broadcasting put under control of Communications Ministry.
1928		Stalin dominant in USSR.
1931		Japan takes over Chinese province of Manchuria.
1932		Japanese Ministry of Education sets up Bureau of Thought Supervision.
1933		German Press Law brings press under government control.
	30 January	Hitler appointed Chancellor of Germany.
	13 March	Goebbels heads German Reich Ministry for Enlightenment and Propaganda.
	23 March	German Enabling Law gives Hitler great deal of personal power.
	14 July	Nazis declared the only legal party in Germany.
	2 August	Hitler proclaimed Führer (leader).
1935		Army officer made Minister of Education in Japan.
	15 March	Germany openly rearming.
1936		Nazis use Berlin Olympics as a propaganda opportunity.
	3 March	Britain increases defence expenditure.
	8 March	German troops enter Rhineland.
	18 July	Spanish Civil War begins.
	1 November	Rome-Berlin Axis established.
1937		Italian Propaganda Ministry set up.
	7 July	Japan invades China province of Manchuria.
	6 November	Italy joins Germany and Japan in Anti-Comintern Pact.
1938		Stalin's enemies being purged in USSR.
	4 February	Hitler commander of all German armed forces.
	12 March	*Anschluss* (union) of Germany and Austria declared by Nazis.
	12 August	Crisis in Czechoslovakian province of Sudetenland, containing many Germans German troops mobilize.
	29-30 September	Czechoslovakian crisis defused at Munich Conference.
	10 October	German troops into Sudetenland.

1939		*Confessions of a Nazi Spy* released by US film studio.
	March	End of Spanish Civil War.
	16 March	Czechoslovakia invaded.
	31 March	Britain and France promise to uphold Polish independence.
	18 April	USSR suggests alliance with GB and France, who refuse.
	28 April	Hitler rejects peace proposals from President Roosevelt.
	2 May	Hitler and Mussolini make a 'Pact of Steel': an alliance between their two countries.
	23 August	Nazi-Soviet Non-Aggression Pact signed.
	September	British Ministry of Information formed.
	1 September	Germany invades Poland.
	3 September	Britain and France declare war on Germany.
	17 September	Soviet troops into Poland.
	Autumn	British government launches its disastrous 'Them' and 'Us' poster campaign.
	30 November	USSR invades Finland.
1940		Charlie Chaplin's *The Great Dictator* released.
		'Lord Haw-Haw' broadcasting from Germany to a large audience in Britain.
	9 April	German army attacks Norway and Denmark.
	10 May	German army attacks Holland, France and Belgium.
		Churchill replaces Neville Chamberlain as prime minister.
	26 May	Beginning of Dunkirk evacuation.
	June	Battle of Britain begins (ends September).
	10 June	Mussolini declares war on Britain and France.
	22 June	France surrender signed.
	August	President Roosevelt establishes Office of Government Reports and Coordinator of Inter-American Affairs to help with US propaganda.
	14 September	Italy invades Egypt.
	27 September	Japan, Germany and Italy form Tripartite Pact.
	28 October	Italy invades Greece.
	5 November	Roosevelt re-elected president of USA.

1941		Roosevelt establishes Office of the Coordinator of Information.
	January	British government closes *Daily Worker* and *Week* (which were closed until August 1942).
	9 February	German troops to North Africa.
	Spring	German 'whisper campaign' to disguise the build-up of troops on the Eastern Front.
	11 March	Lend-Lease Act signed, enabling US to give war aid to Britain.
	Summer	Hollywood begins to release a number of interventionist films, eg *A Yank in the RAF*.
	22 June	German invasion of the USSR.
	July	US embargos on sale of oil and steel to Japan.
	August	British Political Warfare Executive set up.
	7 August	Stalin becomes supreme commander of Soviet forces.
	17 October	General Tojo prime minister of Japan.
	November	German forces halted outside Moscow.
	7 December	Japanese attack on Pearl Harbor.
	8 December	USA and Britain declare war on Japan.
	11 December	Germany and Italy declare war on USA.
1942		American Office of the Coordinator of Information becomes Office of Strategic services.
		Japanese Cabinet Information Board set up.
		BBC sets up a Propaganda Unit for domestic broadcasting.
		German film industry nationalized.
	15 February	Singapore falls to Japanese.
	Spring	British government considers closing the *Daily Mirror* and *Sunday Pictorial*. Eventually decides against doing so.
	8 May	US naval success at Battle of Coral Sea (which began 5-6 May).
	4-5 June	Further US naval success at Battle of Midway.
	July	Battle of Stalingrad begins (ends February 1943).
	23 October	British drive back Germans at Battle of El Alamein (ends 4 November).
1943		Tokyo Rose obtaining a large audience among US troops in the Pacific.
	5 July	Beginning of Battle of Kursk; ends 23 August with Soviet victory.
	10 July	Allies land in Sicily.
	25 July	Mussolini resigns.
	3 September	Allies land in Italy; Italy leaves the war.
	13 October	Italy declares war on Germany.
1944	March	Soviet troops enter Poland.
	Spring	Massive Allied leaflet campaign over Nazi Europe.
	6 June	D-Day Allied landings in Normandy.
	23 June	Soviet offensive begins on eastern front.
	6 October	Soviets enter Czechoslovakia and Hungary.
	20 October	US forces land in Philippines.
	November	Unrelenting bombing of Japan begins.
	December	Unsuccessful German offensive in Ardennes.
1945	4 February	Yalta Conference opens.
	1 April	US forces land on Okinawa.
	12 April	Roosevelt dies – Truman becomes president of USA.
	20 April	Russians reach Berlin.
	May	US begins massive leaflet campaign over Japan.
	7 May	Germany surrenders.
	26 June	United Nations formed.
	July	Churchill's Conservative party defeated in general election and Churchill resigns as prime minister
	6 August	Atomic bomb dropped on Hiroshima.
	8 August	USSR declares war on Japan.
	9 August	Atomic bomb dropped on Nagasaki.
	14 August	Japan surrenders.
	October	US Office of Strategic Services abolished. Civil war resumes in China.

Index

Numbers in **bold** refer to both pictures and text.